MEGAMURALS & SUPERGRAPHICS:

Big Art

by Environmental Communications®

Created and Edited by

DAVID GREENBERG
KATHRYN SMITH
STUART TEACHER

Running Press
Philadelphia, Pennsylvania

Copyright © 1977 Running Press. Printed in the United States of America.
All rights reserved under the Pan-American and International Copyright Conventions.

International representatives: Kaimon & Polon, Inc., 2175 Lemoine Avenue, Fort Lee, New Jersey 07024

9 8 7 6 5 4 3 2 1
Digit on right indicates the number of this printing.

Library of Congress Cataloging in Publication Data
Environmental Communications® (Firm).
   Big art.
   1. Street art—United States.   2. Mural painting
and decoration—20th century—United States. I. Title.
ND2608.E58 1977   751.7'3'0973   77-14043
ISBN 0-89471-006-0 pbk.   ISBN 0-89471-007-9 lib. bdg.

*Environmental Communications® distributes slides,
films, videotapes, and books on architecture, design,
and art. For a copy of their catalogue send $3.75 to
64 Windward Avenue, Venice, California 90291.*

Cover and interior design by James Wizard Wilson

Cover photo by Steve Axelrad:
*"The Isle of California." The Los Angeles Fine Arts
Squad. 1970–71. Butler Avenue, Los Angeles.*

Back cover photo:
*"Nut-And-Bolt." Paul Levy. 1972. Plum
Street and West 4th Street, Cincinnati.*

Typography: Korinna and Caledonia, by The Kingswood Group, Ardmore, Pennsylvania
Printed by Pearl Pressman Liberty, Philadelphia, Pennsylvania

This book may be ordered directly from the publisher.
Please include 25 cents postage.
Try your bookstore first.

Running Press
38 South Nineteenth Street
Philadelphia, Pennsylvania 19103

INTRODUCTION

David Greenberg

The mural movement is one of the most positive and beautiful legacies of the spirit and change of the '60s. Psychedelic art never survived, but street paintings did, and now they adorn what were once some of the dreariest walls in practically every major city in North America.

These works can be identified with both the technique of early twentieth century Mexican muralists, who painted freely on the wall, and the more sophisticated technological methods of modern commercial billboard painters. It can be said that all of today's big art stems from one or the other of these traditions.

Though most styles can probably be seen in most places, Los Angeles, San Francisco, New

"Flamingo Hilton." Foster and Kleiser. 1973. Sunset Strip, Los Angeles.
A billboard hovering over the Sunset Strip beckons motorists to a Las Vegas hotel.

York, Montreal, Santa Fe, Chicago, Cincinnati, and other major cities all have their own particular character. And for good reason—the large vertical abstract paintings of New York done by the City Walls group would look a little incongruous on the Sunset Strip, just as the beautiful pastoral scenes in the Midwest would probably be mistaken for health food restaurants if they were in San Francisco. But somehow, though they are all so different, there is an uncanny sameness about these paintings. And that comes from their roots in our culture— not the kind of culture we identify with museums, but the kind that is found in the media and the street.

Why murals? For a long time, many artists

had been totally alienated from museums and galleries. A closed system, begun during the late forties and fifties, had developed around certain important galleries in New York and Los Angeles. Through their critical influences, this powerful establishment dictated a highly specific direction and definition for fine art. In a sense, it was this overwhelming obstacle that forced certain artists, like Vic Henderson of the Los Angeles Fine Arts Squad, into the streets. In many ways, the mural movement of the early '70s was not unlike that of underground films in the '60s—an alternative form reacting

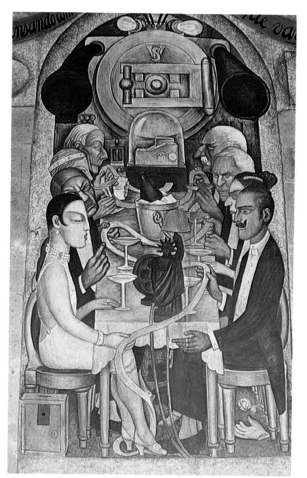 

Untitled. Diego Rivera. 1923–28. Secretariat of Public Education, Mexico City.

Over 250 panels around the balconies of a three-story

against a totally closed system. And street paintings had the added advantage of being even more public and accessible than the established world of art.

The phenomenon of big art has always been of special interest to Environmental Communications. Both seemed to spring upon the scene at the same time and in the same place. And what better place could be found to chart the development of the mural movement? Louis Kahn, one of America's most distinguished architects, once said that "L.A. is truth, whether you like it or not." This makes a lot more sense when you

building document the history of Mexico in the twentieth century up until the time of the revolution.

understand that Kahn's definition of truth is *people:* what people believe and think and feel is what is important, what is true.

In Los Angeles, those inner workings are visually obvious. Expressions of personal aesthetics are everywhere, from custom paint jobs on cars and vans to houses painted in favorite colors. The truth of the barrio is on its walls in the form of graffiti and murals which can be traced back to the traditional style of the old Mexican masters like Orozco, Siqueros, and Rivera. The truth of our culture also seems apparent on the large-scale painted billboards of the Sunset Strip.

So, since this is basically a book about people's art, this is basically a book about people. And *Big Art* is basically the story of big truth.

ACKNOWLEDGEMENTS

Kathryn Smith

Unlike gallery and museum paintings, street art is more important in its day-to-day interaction with people than in the weighty documentation that frequently accompanies institutionalized art. Yet because muralists often receive little pay, it seems even more important to give them proper credit. These photographs were taken under a variety of circumstances by a variety of different people. It was not always possible to obtain documentation at the time the mural was photographed. In many instances, information has been gathered after the fact, by contacting either a mural resource center, the owner or patron of the mural, or the artists themselves. In some instances, it was impossible to obtain

"McDonald's Hamburgers." Foster and Kleiser. 1972. Foster and Kleiser Company, Los Angeles.
The effect of the giant hamburger is the result of thousands of man hours spent over a period of months creating the essence of "juice," not grease.

any information at all. In this case, when either an artist or a date could not be identified, it is listed as "unknown."

Like mural painting itself, this book has been a work of collaboration. Many people have given generously of their time and shared both their knowledge and enthusiasm for the contemporary mural movement. Special thanks must be extended to the photographers. To John Bright, for his thorough documentation of the West Coast, especially San Francisco and the Chicano murals of East Los Angeles. To Roger Webster, for his unique contribution as a member of Environmental Communications in his coverage of West and East Coast murals, particularly those in and around Los Angeles. To On the Wall Productions for their documentations of the Midwest mural movement. And to the other individuals who have contributed to the remainder of the book: Susan Einstein, Mark Rogovin, the Chicago Mural Group, Joel Peter Witkin, Robert Bryan, Steve Axelrad, Bill Weiner, Marlo Wolfe, Leyba Guzman, Susan Sullivan, Gary Greenberg, Rick Bednarek, H. L. Dufresne, Leonard Koren, Gene Young, Dee D'Orazio, Tom Sewell, David Greenberg, S.I.T.E., Jack Frost, Kathleen Greenberg, Sharon Peckinpah, Foster & Kleiser, Robert Landau, Mark Rennie and Diane Hall.

Generous thanks also to the many individuals and organizations who have provided information on *Big Art:*

In Los Angeles: Vic Henderson, Kent Twitchell, the County of Los Angeles, Wayne Holwick, Simone Posthuma, Wayne Healy, John Bright, David Kunzle, Deena Metzger, and Mura Bright.

In San Francisco: Susan Einstein, Jim Buffalo, the Neighborhood Arts–San Francisco Art Commission, Marine World, and the California Department of Transportation.

In the Midwest: Sarah Lindquist and Bob Fishbone, On the Wall Productions, St. Louis; the Parks and Recreations Department, Columbus, Indiana; the Valspar Corporation and the Schmitt Music Center, Minneapolis, Minnesota; the Public Art Workshop and the Chicago Mural Group, Chicago.

On the East Coast: Doris Freedman, City Walls, and Susan Caruso-Green, the City Arts Workshop, New York; the Institute of Contemporary Art, Boston.

In Canada: Benson & Hedges, and M. Lavalguy, City of Montreal.

Special mention should be made of several individuals at Environmental Communications who have aided in documentation: Elizabeth Freeman, Sheri Tanibata, Susan Sullivan, and Marlo Wolfe.

Notwithstanding the above contributions, any errors or oversights are the responsibility of the authors.

"This Building Isn't Here." Public Works—a Construction Company. Date unknown. Yellow Springs, Ohio.

"Hog Heaven." Les Grimes and Arno Jordan. 1957 to present. Farmer John Brand, Clougherty Meat Packing Company, Los Angeles.

We are taken back to an idyllic era of life on a pig farm, or "hog heaven," where pigs lead a charmed life until the day they end up in the "smokehouse," a metaphor for the reality which lies behind the painting itself. The pigs frolic in believable and unbelievable ways—rolling in mud, eating their fill, peering into windows of the real-life plant which at times enters into and becomes a part of the illusionary landscape. Les Grimes, who had worked as a scenic artist for the movie studios, devoted his

attention to every loving detail of the porcine panorama until 1968 when, completing an area of sky in the great farmland vista, he fell fifty feet from a scaffold to his death. Following Grimes, Arno Jordan, an Austrian immigrant like his predecessor, was hired to continue and maintain the unfinished murals.

Untitled. Richard Anuszkiewicz.
Sponsored by City Walls. 1972.
YWCA, 50th Street and 8th Avenue,
New York.

"Sun and Moon." Artist unknown. 1972. Montreal.

"Work, Education and Struggle: Seeds for Progressive Change." City Arts Workshop. 1975. Delancey Street, New York.

Untitled. California Department of Transportation. 1970. Waldo Grade Tunnel, Marin, California.

On assignment to improve a state highway by painting the concrete green, a supervisor had a rainbow design made up to cover the tunnel entrance. It sat in his office for ten months before he decided to commit the state to this unprecedented form of beautification.

"Muriel." On the Wall Productions. 1974. Volks and Vans, 5645 Manchester, St. Louis.

This mural of a frog eating "bugs" was painted on the side of a Volkswagen repair shop in exchange for a rebuilt van.

Untitled. James Doman, Jr. Date unknown. 225th Street, New York.

The outside of an architect's office suggests the blueprint of his planned renovation.

"Dynamo, Surge and Phoenix."
Jason Crum. Sponsored by City
Walls. 1970–71. Hart Island,
Bronx, New York.

Untitled. Chris Rocha. 1977.
Warren Sound Studios,
Highland Avenue, Los Angeles.

Untitled. Richard Haas. Sponsored by City Walls.
1975. Greene Street and Prince Street, New York.
Only after a double take does the viewer realize that
just one facade of this building is real.

*"Ghost Town." Los Angeles Fine
Arts Squad. 1973. Conejo Security
Bank, Thousand Oaks, California.*
Painted on a bank, this vision
of the future of the San
Fernando Valley shows a ghost
town in which the ecological
and financial consequences of
the present have returned the
valley to its original state—a
barren and deserted sheep
grazing frontier.

"I Am the People." Caryl Yasko with Celia Radek and James Yanagisawa. 1974. 2659 North Milwaukee, Chicago.

A complex and richly symbolic mural designed to relate to the predominantly Eastern European residents of the Logan Square neighborhood. It represents humanity (a family of man, woman and child) in a continuing struggle for the basic ingredients of survival with forces (bureaucracy, big business, etc.) beyond their control. These are symbolized in the large wheel—Food, Clothing, Shelter—and in the four smaller wheels—Recreation, Work, Religion and Education. This wall became so admired by the community that it was declared better than the wall by Chagall downtown which was dedicated at the same time.

"The Builders." John Weber and Celia Radek. 1975. 2840 North Ashland, Chicago. The building belongs to a construction rental company which provides scaffolding for the muralists.

"Phoenix." City Arts Workshop. 1976. 42nd Street and 8th Avenue, New York.

"Monument to Strother Martin."
Kent Twitchell. 1971–72. Fountain
and Kingsley, Hollywood.
Twitchell started this work with a
likeness of an actor on a "Wild
Bunch" movie poster and, as word
of the mural spread, Strother Martin
himself came to check it out and
stayed to pose.

"Steve McQueen." Kent Twitchell. 1971.
12th and Union Avenue, Los Angeles.

Untitled. Kent Twitchell. 1971–72. Monterey Park,
California. [Destroyed]

Untitled. Michael Rios. 1971.
Neighborhood Legal Assistance,
Mission District, San Francisco.
Inspired by the cartoon, *El
Topo,* this mural in fourteen
scenes is drawn from the
neighborhood experience of the
artist: waiting for food stamps,
at the doctor's office, going to
work. The Mission residents are
depicted as moles leading an
underground life, the
authorities as pigs and hound
dogs.

"Gods of Pegana." David Russell and the Inner City Mural Program. 1974. Olympic and Figueroa, Los Angeles. The three gods are Mung, representing "the end;" Sagan, holding a staff, symbolizing both "peace" and "war;" and Cyrena, who stands for "life."

Untitled. Artist unknown. Date unknown. Full Circle Boutique, Culver Boulevard, Los Angeles. [Destroyed]

"Latinoamerica." Mujeres
*Muralistas. 1974. Mission
Model Cities, Mission and 25th,
San Francisco.*
One of the few murals painted
exclusively by women.

*Untitled. Jane Golden and the Citywide Mural
Project. 1975. Ocean Park Boulevard and Main
Street, Santa Monica.*

"Lips." Animation Design. 1972. Rue Jeane-Marc and Avenue du President Kennedy, Montreal.

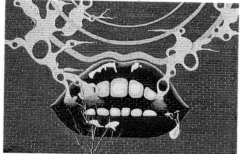

"Tower of Power." *Rudilo Guielerno a[nd]
Jack Frost. 1975. Valencia Gardens
Housing Project, 18th and Lexington, S[an]
Francisco.*

"Lucas Valley View." *Hilaire L.
Dufresne. 1975. Lucas Valley, Marin,
California.*
This mural was painted at the site of t[he]
abandoned Clover Dairy on a remaini[ng]
section of concrete paving. Its aerial v[iew]
of the valley in which the dairy is loca[ted]
can only be seen from the surrounding
hills.

"Venice in the Snow." The Los Angeles Fine Arts Squad. 1970. 18th and Speedway, Venice, California. [Obscured]
This scene depicts a site along the beach on Ocean Front Walk, complete with well-known local characters. The photographic realism was juxtaposed with a surrealistic touch—it never snows in Southern California. After two years, a four-unit apartment house was constructed only inches away from this local landmark, in spite of active community protest.

Untitled. Tania. Sponsored by City Walls. 1970. Mercer and 3rd streets, New York.

Untitled. Eugene Greenland, Ray Vanderhagen, Leonard Castellanos, Gerry Cabazos, and Tomas Gonzales. Sponsored by the Mechicano Art Center. 1973. Glendale Boulevard, Los Angeles. These murals replaced graffiti on a stairway across from Echo Park Lake in a Chicano neighborhood of the same name.

"Groupie." Wayne Holwick. 1968. Hart Avenue and Neilson Avenue, Venice, California. [Destroyed]
Known as the first "hip" wall mural in Venice, "Groupie" was created when Holwick simply walked up to a wall one day and started painting.

"Rimbaud." Wayne Holwick. 1976. Hart and Nielson, Santa Monica. [Destroyed]
After the painting of the "Groupie" was whitewashed, the artist replaced it with an image that had been haunting him. Using paint and ashes from the fireplace, he executed the entire portrait at once.

"Maurice Ravel's 'Gaspard de la Nuit.'" Lawrence Sign Company. 1972. Schmitt Music Center, 88 South 10th Street, Minneapolis.

"Miro Fantasy." Carlos Basanta, Martin Vines, and I. A. Brown. 1972. "Mothers," Boulevard de Maisonneuve at Crescent, Montreal.
Two walls above an outdoor cafe in the style of the Spanish painter, Joan Miro.

"Liberty and Education."
Los Artes Guadalupanos
de Aztlan. 1972. St.
Francis Drive, Santa Fe.
A powerful mural by a
group of artists, several
from the same family,
who came together in
1971 to commemorate the
death of one of their
young brothers from an
overdose of drugs.

Untitled. Los Artes
Guadalupanos de Aztlan.
1971–72. Santa Fe
Janitorial Service Co-op,
632 Agua Fria Street,
Santa Fe.

"The Black Athlete Arises." Calumet High School Art Club, with Barry Bruner. 1973. Auburn YMCA, 1155 81st Street, Chicago.

Untitled. Japantown community children. c. 1974–75. Japantown, San Francisco.

"Para El Mercada" ("For the Market"). Mujeres Muralistas. 1975. Paco's Tacos, South Van Ness and 24th, San Francisco.
This mural was commissioned by the owner of a foodstand for the wall adjacent to his parking lot. It depicts in bright and luscious colors a market day in the life of a tropical village.

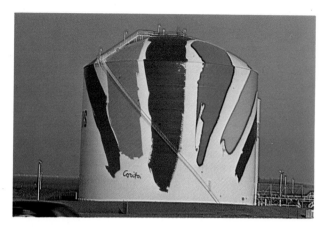

*Untitled. Corita Kent. 1971. Boston Gas
Company, Boston.*

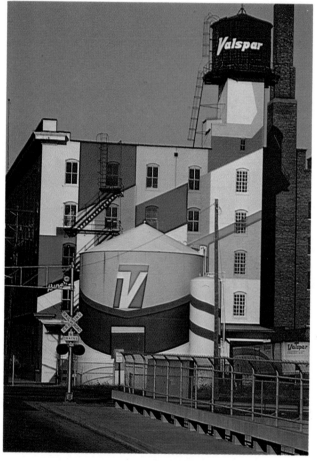

*"Demolition." Peter Busa. 1973. Valspar
Corporation, 1101 3rd Street,
Minneapolis.*

Untitled. Randy Kirk and Robert Burnett. 1975. Lincoln Park, Columbus, Indiana. These designs, winners of an urban wall contest, appear on the end walls of a handball court.

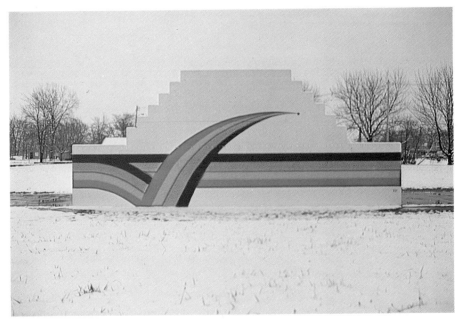

Untitled. Randy Kirk and Robert Burnett. 1975. Lincoln Park, Columbus, Indiana. Kirk and Burnett were high school students when they produced the designs on these handball courts.

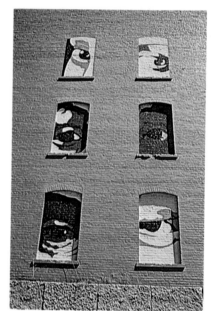

"Eyes." Preston McClanahan.
Sponsored by Urban Walls. 1972.
Elm Street between West 3rd and
4th streets, Cincinnati.

"Realflectoism." On the Wall
Productions. 1975. Young and
Evray, Dallas.
Commissioned by a local
businessman, this painting
shows the downtown area with
a new city hall in construction.
The building's owner is seen
walking down the street.

"Kosherilla." Tom Strohmaier.
1972. Temple Delicatessen,
Cincinnati.
One of Urban Walls' most
lighthearted murals is in
downtown Cincinnati—a
mythical gorilla partial to
kosher pickles hangs around his
local deli.

"Silhouettes-On-The-Shade."
Tom Smith. 1972. Cincinnati.

Untitled. La Regeneracion. 1972. City Terrace,
Eastern Avenue and Comly Drive, Los Angeles.

"Plumed Serpent." Willie Herron. 1972.
Alley off Miller Avenue, Los Angeles.

*"Rainbow People." Haight-Ashbury Muralists.
1972–74. Haight between Ashbury and Masonic, San
Francisco.*

This very-well known mural was so important to the
community that it was repainted in the same
location when the original began to deteriorate.
First to commemorate a peace march against the
war in Vietnam, it depicts a vision of the new
America which could be a result of the People's
Movement. In the center, musicians—who used to
play free concerts in the park—jam at the source of
two brilliant rainbows. Behind them, an Indian
peers over a flaming horizon, recalling this nation's
native peoples. The rainbow to the left arches over
community residents marching behind the San

Francisco Mime Troupe down an unlittered, car-free
Haight Street. In the foreground, people of many
ages and races cluster happily around an octopus
they've overcome. It bears the faces of Nixon, Ford
and Rockefeller, while its tentacles—many of them
severed—clutch symbols of what the muralists see
hurting America: a heroin syringe, an Air Force
bomber, a Watergate tape, an eviction notice, a
grocery bag full of money, and a vacuum nozzle
sucking dollars from Third World continents. The
right hand rainbow bursts over a visionary image of
San Francisco and ends in a fist denoting liberation.
Here the Golden Gate Bridge leads to a communal
organic garden where children romp beside the park
merry-go-round.

"Windansea Boutique." Artist unknown. Date unknown. La Jolla, California.

"The Aquarius Theater."
The Fool. 1969. Sunset
Boulevard, Hollywood.
[Destroyed]

"Pink House." Environmental
Communications. 1969. Venice,
California. [Destroyed]
The first home of Environmental
Communications was a small stucco
bungalow on the beach, and one of
the group's first projects was for
each to take a brush and start
painting.

"Brooks Street." The Los Angeles Fine Arts Squad. 1969. Brooks Street at Pacific Avenue, Venice, California. [Unfinished]
This was the first painting executed by the Los Angeles Fine Arts Squad, which believes that art should not be the exclusive property of galleries, museums and collectors. From the very beginning, their work has dealt with alterations in the perception of reality—in this instance, the painting is a mirror image of the view directly behind the viewer when he is facing the wall mural. The squad left this mural unfinished to start the mammoth task of painting the Climax Club, their largest work to date.

"Brandelli's Brig." Arthur Mortimer and friends.
1973. Brandelli's Brig, West Washington Boulevard,
Venice, California.

A painting within a painting, this mural depicts the
owners of a local bar posing beside their place and,
in the background, the muralist painting them.

". . . to the Horse Trough." On the Wall Productions. 1976. Carondelet, St. Louis.

"Hippie Knowhow." The Los Angeles Fine Arts Squad. 1971. Parc Florale, Château de Vincente, Paris, France.

Commissioned by the French government to do a wall painting for the Paris Biennial, the Los Angeles Fine Arts Squad created an illusion of themselves painting a wall.

"The Isle of California." The Los Angeles Fine Arts Squad. 1970–71. Butler Avenue, Los Angeles.

One of the jokes familiar to all Southern Californians is that someday a cataclysmic earthquake will occur along the Arizona-Nevada border that will send California floating out into the Pacific Ocean— and as a consequence, beachfront property will be for sale in Phoenix.

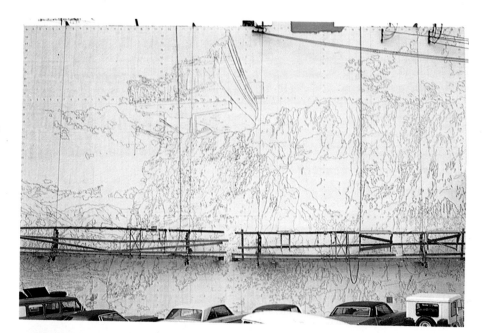

"Solarcarte." Paul Whitehead. Sponsored by the Eyes and Ears Foundation. 1977. Hayworth and Sunset, Los Angeles. [Removed]

"Midge and Madge." D.J. Hall and A. Wilf. Sponsored by the Eyes and Ears Foundation. 1977. Santa Monica and La Cienega, Los Angeles. [Removed]
All the *Eyes and Ears* billboards were so large that they had to be painted in a movie studio rented especially for the project.

"Pat-Tap." Bill Tunberg. Sponsored by the Eyes and Ears Foundation. 1977. Holloway and La Cienega, Los Angeles. [Removed]
This is a difficult billboard to comprehend from a moving car since it explores words that read backwards and forwards combined with female forms. The meaning of the seminude figure crawling toward the caboose of a train is unclear.

"How to Draw." Karen Carson. Sponsored by the Eyes and Ears Foundation. 1977. Santa Monica and La Cienega boulevards, Los Angeles.

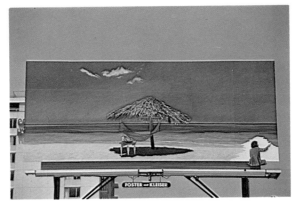

"Cat Stevens." Foster and Kleiser. 1973. Los Angeles.

"Back of Hollywood." Ed Ruscha. 1977. Wilshire Boulevard across from the Los Angeles County Museum of Art, Los Angeles. [Removed]
Ruscha reversed his famous pop art portrait of the real estate sign which still hovers in the hills over Hollywood, making it possible to properly view the painting-on-billboard only through a moving car's rearview mirror.

"Indeterminate Facade." S.I.T.E. (Sculpture in the Environment). 1974–75. Almeda-Genoa Shopping Center, Kingspoint and Kleckley Streets, Houston. This contemporary construction was designed to startle viewers.

"The Richmond Peel." S.I.T.E. (Sculpture in the Environment). 1971. Best Products, Midlothian Turnpike, Richmond.
This appliance store with a peeling facade is constructed of brick and a special high-test mortar. A state trooper, believing it was unsafe, attempted to evacuate the building.

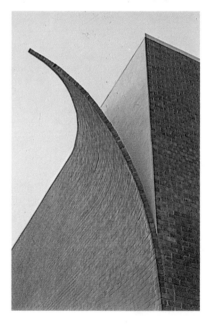

*"Viet Nam Tiger Cages—Free All
Political Prisoners." Mark Rogovin and
Holly Highfill. 1974. Clergy and Laity
Concerned, Chicago.*
A street theater prop used in a
demonstration against the Vietnam war.

*"(The Black Submarine) Robert E.
LeRoi." The Los Angeles Fine Arts Squad.
1971. Balboa Bay, Newport Beach,
California. [Removed]*
Intended to startle, this is a full size
reproduction in two dimensions of a
World War II Japanese submarine.

"Lindy Squared." On the Wall Productions. 1977. 10th and Chestnut Streets, St. Louis.
This computerized image of Charles A. Lindbergh took two years to design and one week to paint. The mural is an exercise in visual perception since the 1160 square blocks of 70 shades of gray blend together to form the portrait as the passerby moves away from it.

"Wally." On the Wall Productions. 1974. 8th and Pine, St. Louis.
Painted "Tom Sawyer" style by a group of friends for the cost of materials, this mural was affectionately nicknamed because it was on such a large wall.

"Lightning." Sarro. 1973. Ste. Catherine and Ste. Dominique, Montreal.

Untitled. Artist unknown. 1972–73. Montreal.

*"Dreams of Flight." David Botello. 1973.
Estrada Courts Housing Project, Olympic
Boulevard and Lorena Street, Los
Angeles.*
One of the most joyous Chicano murals
depicts the artist's fantasies of flying—
from swinging on an old tire tied to a
tree, to riding a winged horse, to
astronauts landing on the moon.

*Untitled. Toltecas en Aztlan. 1974.
Balboa Park, San Diego.*
A converted water tank houses offices,
workrooms, studios and a theater.

"Hermano, por que?" David Lopez and the Arizona Mara Gang. 1973. Maravilla Housing Project, Brooklyn and Mednik Avenues, Los Angeles. [Moved]

A gang-inspired mural on the walls of a housing project became a local shrine that eventually received a blessing from the Vatican. This tribute to a young member who had died reads: "Brother, and why are we here on earth without bleeding, without walking. Brother, why?" The residents responded by placing candles and flowers at its base every day, and also at a companion mural of Our Lady of Guadalupe.

Untitled. Carlito Gaegos. 1973. Estrada Courts Housing Project, Olympic Boulevard and Lorena Street, Los Angeles. [Destroyed]

Untitled. Vatos del Maravilla. 1973. Four Square Auto Wreckers, 304 North Ford at Michigan, Los Angeles.

This mural was designed and painted by an East Los Angeles gang.

Untitled. Les P'tits Soleil: Guite. 1972–73. Montreal.

"Wall of Meditation." On the Wall Productions. 1976. Grand and Shenandoah, St. Louis.

"Environmental Response." On the Wall Productions. 1975. Lake and Waterman, St. Louis.

"Earthrise." Public Works—a Construction Company. Date unknown. Yellow Springs, Ohio.

"Two Faces on Barn." Public Works—a Construction Company. Date unknown. Yellow Springs, Ohio.

Untitled. Gil Hernandez. 1973. Estrada Courts Housing Project, Olympic Boulevard and Lorena Street, Los Angeles.

"New Birth." City Arts Workshop. 1974. Chrysty and Rivington streets, New York.

Untitled. Artist unknown. Date unknown. Northern California.
An official United States Post Office.

Untitled. Public Works—a Construction Company. Date unknown. Yellow Springs, Ohio.
A mural painted by a communications class at Antioch College for the College Volunteer Fire Department.

Untitled. Todd McKie. 1969. 141 Merrimac, Boston.

Untitled. Allan D'Arcangelo. 1970. 218 West 64th Street, New York.
D'Arcangelo was one of the first New York gallery artists to become interested in street art. As early as 1965 he was painting fireplugs and by June, 1967, he produced one of the first professional wall paintings in New York.

"View from Around the Bend." Public Works—a Construction Company. Date unknown. Yellow Springs, Ohio.

This painting by a communications class at Antioch College mirrors the view down the town's main thoroughfare at sunset.

Untitled. Alvin Loving.
Sponsored by City Walls. 1973.
103 West 42nd Street, New
York.

Untitled. Tania. 1967. 10
Evergreen Avenue, Brooklyn,
New York.
The first professional
noncommercial outdoor wall
painting in New York was
designed as part of a program
to convert ten debris-laden
vacant lots into vest-pocket
parks.

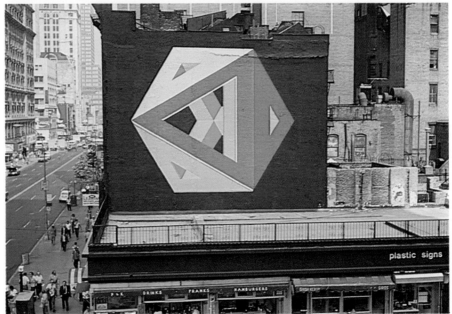

Untitled. Mike Boll. c. 1972–73. Marine World— Africa, USA, San Francisco.

Untitled. Artist unknown. 1972–73. Montreal.

"The Beverly Hills Siddhartha." The Los Angeles Fine Arts Squad. 1969–70. Climax II, La Cienega Boulevard, Los Angeles. [Destroyed]

One of the first contemporary narrative paintings, this mural depicts the spiritual journey of a young man from the crass materialism of Beverly Hills to a realization of inner peace and beauty. The painting was commissioned by a discotheque owner in order to attract attention to his club on a busy commercial strip. The painting reads from left to right. Siddhartha is seen leaving his family home in Beverly Hills against the background of a torn-out section of a tourist's map of the movie stars' homes.

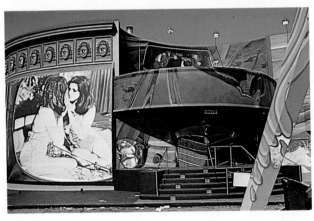

The next two panels show Siddhartha's education and discovery depicted on television screens. As he leaves, he is admonished by a television commercial to be "security minded." The next panel shows a very erotic and narcissistic girl touching her own reflection in a mirror. Siddhartha and the erotic girl arrive at the Climax II nightclub driving a Mercedes Benz, a symbol of the decadent, hedonistic life. He rejects this life of total sensuality and flees the nightclub. He is next found sitting in a stream meditating. The story concludes with Siddhartha, a humble artist, painting a girl's image as he sits in his modest hut by the seashore. These iconographic images of the '60s youth's disillusion with "established values," like those of the art galleries and museums which

originally sent the Los Angeles Fine Arts Squad out into the streets, became world famous in the two years they could be seen on La Cienega. When the club changed hands, the new owner wanted a different image and had the walls whitewashed.

"Que Sera, Seurat?" On the Wall Productions. 1976. Grand and Arsenal, St. Louis.
Across the street from Tower Grove Park is a beautiful garden with gazebos. Its turn-of-the-century images are reflected in a mural which derives its style from pointillism, a movement made famous by the French painter Georges Seurat.

Untitled. Stefano Falk. 1966. La Strada Restaurant, Los Feliz Boulevard, Los Angeles.
La Strada means "the street," and the owner wanted his restaurant to be reminiscent of the streets of old Rome.

*Untitled. Jim Sol. 1976. Santa Monica
Pier Merry-Go-Round, Santa Monica.*

*Untitled. Willie Herron. 1972. Alley near
East City Terrace Drive, Los Angeles.*

"Ghosts of the Barrio." Wayne Healy. 1974.
Ramona Gardens Housing Project, Los Angeles.
Four *vatos locos* (street dudes) and their three
ancestors—an American Indian, a Spanish
conquistador, and a Mexican of the revolutionary
period—ask the question, "Where do we go from
here?"

*"Positively 4th Street." John
Wherle and John Rampley.
1976. DeYoung Museum, San
Francisco.*
A vision of San Francisco from
a prominent point along the
freeway, with a view of the
skyline crumbling in the
background. The city,
abandoned by its residents, has
been taken over by wild
animals, many of them on the
endangered species list.

*Untitled. Keith Tucker. 1973.
Bug Builders, 1423 6th Street,
Santa Monica.*
A repair shop agreed to service
the artist's car in exchange for
a mural.

"Two Girls." Wayne Holwick. 1970. Los Angeles. [Destroyed]

"Trinity." Kent Twitchell. 1977. Otis Art Institute, Wilshire Boulevard, Los Angeles. [In progress]
This contemporary Trinity will consist of Billy Gray, the son on the TV series, "Father Knows Best," as Christ; Jan Clayton, the mother on "Lassie," as the Virgin Mary; and Clayton Moore, the original Lone Ranger, as God—because no one ever saw the face of the Lone Ranger.

"The Old Woman of the Freeway." Kent Twitchell. *Sponsored by the Inner City Mural Program. 1974. Hollywood Freeway, Los Angeles.*

One of Twitchell's most universally acclaimed pieces shows the face of Lillian Bronson, who played as a regular on the "Perry Mason Show." Twitchell picks film personalities as subjects because they will seem familiar to the viewer, who may not, however, recall exactly why.

"Venice High Yearbook, Class of '53." Arthur Mortimer. *1970. Venice, California.*

Untitled. Jack Frost. 1975. Valencia Gardens Housing Project, 18th and Lexington, San Francisco.
Two hot air balloons rise out of a canyon, one decorated with the eagle insignia of the United Farm Workers and the other with the flag of Mexico.

"Come Together Each in Your Own Perceiving of Yourself." Ruby Newman and Selma Brown. 1975–76. Public Library, Page near Cole, San Francisco.

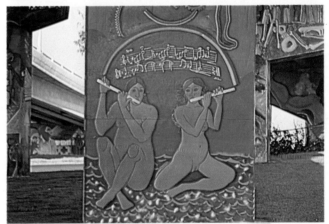

Untitled. Toltecas en Aztlan. 1973–74. People's Park, San Diego.
Barrio residents were offended by the intrusion of a freeway in their neighborhood and responded by creating this outdoor art gallery.

"Ribbons." Mur-a-Mur Squad. 1972. Rue de Vitre, Rue de Bullion, Avenue de Hotel-de-Ville, Montreal.
The purple-orange stripe represents the trans-Canadian auto route, which bisects the country.

F I N I S

INVENTORY 1983